CAPE TOWN

ANDREW LANGLEY

WORLD ALMANAC® LIBRARY

Please visit our web site at: www.worldalmanaclibrary.com
For a free color catalog describing World Almanac® Library's list of high-quality books
and multimedia programs, call 1-800-848-2928 (USA) or 1-800-387-3178 (Canada).
World Almanac® Library's fax: (414) 332-3567.

Library of Congress Cataloging-in-Publication Data

Langley, Andrew.
    Cape Town / by Andrew Langley.
       p. cm. — (Great cities of the world)
    Includes bibliographical references and index.
    ISBN 0-8368-5045-9 (lib. bdg.)
    ISBN 0-8368-5205-2 (softcover)
    1. Cape Town (South Africa)—Juvenile literature. I. Title. II. Series.
DT2405.C364L36 2005
968.73'55—dc22   2004058989

First published in 2005 by
World Almanac® Library
330 West Olive Street, Suite 100
Milwaukee, WI 53212 USA

Copyright © 2005 by World Almanac® Library.

Produced by Discovery Books
Editors: Kathryn Walker and Kathryn Walker
Series designers: Laurie Shock, Keith Williams
Designer and page production: Keith Williams
Photo researcher: Rachel Tisdale
Diagrams: Keith Williams
Maps: Stefan Chabluk
World Almanac® Library editorial direction: Mark J. Sachner
World Almanac® Library editor: Gini Holland
World Almanac® Library art direction: Tammy West
World Almanac® Library graphic design: Scott M. Krall
World Almanac® Library production: Jessica Morris

Photo credits: AKG Images: p. 12; AKG Images/Ullstein bild: p. 27; Corbis/Reuters: p. 14; Corbis/Gallo
Images/Richard du Tolt: p. 26; Getty Images/AFP: p. 36; Getty Images/AFP/Rajesh Jantilal: p. 17; Getty
Images/AFP/Anna Zieminski: pp. 34, 43; Getty Images/The Image Bank/Laurence Hughes: p. 7; Getty
Images/The Image Bank/Frans Lemmens: p. 15; Getty Images/Per-Anders Petterson: p. 18; Getty Images/
The Image Bank/Andreas Stirnberg: p. 4; Getty Images/Touchline: p. 39; Mary Evans Picture Library: p. 10;
Panos/Eric Miller: p. 22; Still Pictures: pp. 25, 38; Still Pictures/Roger de la Harpe: pp. 24, 33; Still
Pictures/Peter Hirth: pp. 30, 42; Trip: p. 16; Trip/M.Barlow: p. 29; Trip: Penni Bickle: p. 23; Trip/Shaun
Harris: p. 21; Trip/J. Mann: p. 32; Trip/Andria Massey: p. 41; Trip/Robin Smith: cover and title page;
Trip/A. Tovy: p. 13; Trip/Hein Van Harsten: p. 8.

Cover caption: Set on the Cape Peninsula, one of the most southerly points of Africa, Cape Town looks
out on the Atlantic Ocean and enjoys a dramatic setting that makes it one of the most beautiful cities in
the world.

Printed in Canada

1 2 3 4 5 6 7 8 9 09 08 07 06 05

Contents

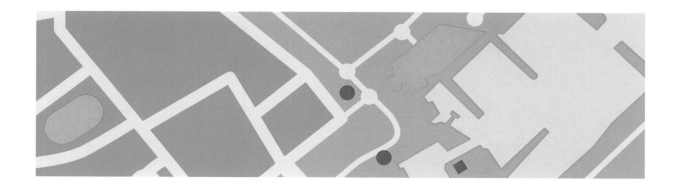

Introduction

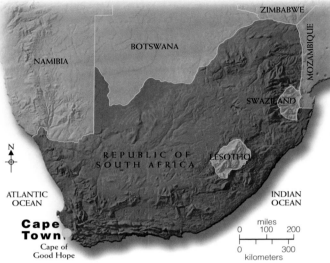

S pread across its stunning seaside location beneath Table Mountain, Cape Town is one of the most beautiful and lively cities in the world and South Africa's most popular tourist attraction. South Africans call Cape Town their "Mother City." It is the home of the country's Parliament and the legislative (lawmaking) capital of South Africa, which is divided into nine provincial areas. The capital of Western Cape Province, Cape Town is an important center of commerce and industry, bustling with a busy international airport, railroad and long-distance bus links, and one of the country's major ports.

◀ *Great natural beauty dominated by the majestic Table Mountain surrounds Cape Town, the oldest city in South Africa.*

The Setting

The city is perched above a hook-shaped peninsula of land on South Africa's west coast and looks out over the Atlantic Ocean. One of the most southerly points of the African continent, this peninsula is called the Cape of Good Hope. At its tip, about 25 miles (40 kilometers) from Cape Town, stretches the rocky and narrow Cape Point, with the Indian Ocean on the east and the Atlantic Ocean on the west.

Table Mountain towers over Cape Town. Surrounded by steep cliffs and gorges, this flat-topped giant rises to a height of more than 3,300 feet (1,000 meters). The city's center lies in a bowl formed by the northern slopes of the mountain—hence the nickname "City Bowl." Large suburban areas stretch from the northeast around to the south. On the west side of the mountain are smaller suburbs and magnificent white sandy beaches pounded by the Atlantic Ocean's waves. Further south lie lush vineyards and the unspoiled Cape Peninsula National Park.

Climate

With its warm dry summers, cool wet winters, and few extremes of weather or temperature, Cape Town enjoys a climate similar to that of San Francisco, California. Since it lies south of the equator, Cape Town's seasons are the opposite of those in northern countries. Spring (from September to November) brings bright sunshine as well as wild winds and storms. The average

January temperature is 70° Fahrenheit (21° Celsius). Summer (from December to March) is hot but usually breezy. Autumn (from March to May) is warm and generally calm, while winter (from June to August) brings clouds and rain, although

South Africa's Capitals

South Africa has not just one but three capital cities. Each one is the headquarters of a different part of the country's government. Cape Town is the legislative capital, where Parliament meets and makes the laws. Pretoria is the administrative capital, the center of day-to-day management of the country's affairs, and Bloemfontein is the judicial capital, home of South Africa's most important courts of justice.

The Cape Peninsula

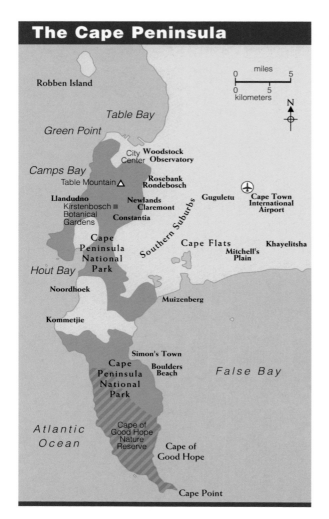

City Center

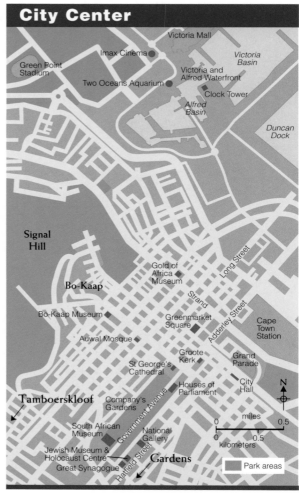

temperatures are still mild. July temperatures average about 54° Fahrenheit (12° C). The city gets 20 inches (51 centimeters) of rain on average each year.

Winds hit Cape Town from nearly every direction during the year. These varying winds mean that the weather around Cape Town can change very quickly, and Capetonians (Cape Town residents) look out for warning signs. For example, if clouds known as "the table cloth" cover Table Mountain, they know that the most famous and persistent wind, the Cape Doctor, is about to start blowing. Blowing from the southeast during summer, the Cape Doctor keeps air pollution at a lower level.

Old and New, Rich and Poor

Cape Town is a place of great contrasts. The downtown area contains grand houses built by European imperialists as well as noisy African markets, modern concrete office

▲ *The recently redeveloped Victoria and Alfred Waterfront is a lively mixture of stores, restaurants, bars, and museums, as well as a working harbor.*

blocks, and the Muslim mosques of the Bo-Kaap district. The massive nineteenth-century dock area has been redeveloped into a highly successful commercial and shopping center. In the bay a few miles to the north lies Robben Island, a prison site during the apartheid era that once held political heroes such as Nelson Mandela, who later became South Africa's first postapartheid president. Now it is a museum.

Even starker is the gulf between rich and poor districts. The Southern Suburbs, which stretch southeast from downtown, are home to many of Cape Town's wealthiest people and the setting for Cape Town University, the Kirstenbosch Botanical Gardens, and vineyards. Beyond them to the south, however, lie the dry and barren plains called Cape Flats, the site of the desolate and often squalid townships where the poorest black and Cape Coloured people live. (In the 1950s, the white government used the term *coloured* as a crude way of defining people who were of mixed black, white, and often Indonesian, Indian, or Malaysian background. The term lingers, although it has less meaning since apartheid has ended.)

The Racial Mix

Few cities contain a more dramatic mixture of peoples than Cape Town, known as the "rainbow city" because its population is made up of many different ethnic groups. Blacks, whites, Cape Coloureds, and people originating from many parts of Asia live here, speaking several different languages and following different cultural patterns. This rich variety can be seen in the vibrant life of the streets, cafés, markets, and clubs, especially downtown.

CHAPTER 1

History of Cape Town

People have lived in the Western Cape for at least thirty thousand years. The earliest people were the San, or Bushmen, who hunted animals and gathered plants for food as they wandered in small groups over southern Africa. They left evidence of their lives in beautiful rock art and cave paintings. Several examples of these have been preserved in the South African Museum in Cape Town's downtown.

Khoikhoi and their Cattle

Little changed in the life of the San until about two thousand years ago, when the Khoikhoi people from the north moved into the area, bringing their herds of sheep and cattle and developing the earliest settled

Rock Paintings

◄ *The San people lived simple lives with few possessions apart from their ostrich shells for carrying water and stone tools and weapons, yet they left behind many beautiful paintings (pictured here) on rocks and in caves. Probably ways of trying to communicate with San ancestors, these usually show hunting expeditions with animals and human figures. The earliest paintings are simply black or brown, but later ones include different colors.*

communities. It seems to have been a peaceful invasion, but the San were still forced to move farther inland to find fresh hunting grounds. From about A.D. 500 onward, new migrants, known as the Bantu-speakers, began moving into southern Africa from the north. One group, the Xhosa, probably made contact with the Khoikhoi to trade and began to settle in the area around the Western and Eastern Capes.

Explorers from Europe

For centuries, Europeans had bought spices, silks, and other precious goods produced in the Far East from overland traders. During the 1420s, the Portuguese decided to look for their own route to the East—which meant finding a way round the huge west coast of Africa and its stormy southern tip and on into the Indian Ocean where they could obtain these items to take back to Europe. No one had ever done this before.

Over the years, bold sailors went gradually farther south. In 1488, Bartholomeu Dias rounded the Cape and came ashore in the calmer seas of Mossel Bay to look for freshwater and food. Relieved and delighted to make a safe landing, Dias gave a Portuguese name to the point—Cabo da Boa Esperanca, or Cape of Good Hope. The way to the Indian Ocean was clear.

The first recorded landing in Table Bay was in 1503. Antonio de Saldanha, a Portuguese admiral, climbed Table Mountain and left his mark by carving a cross—which can still be seen—in the

"The most stately thing and the fairest cape we saw in the whole circumference of the earth."

—Sir Francis Drake, British sailor and circumnavigator, 1580, describing the Cape of Good Hope.

rock at the highest point. His crew, however, got into a fight with the local Khoikhoi that left at least one African dead. A much bloodier incident took place in 1510 when the Khoikhoi killed about seventy-five Portuguese who tried to steal their cattle. In spite of this, the two peoples slowly grew friendlier and began to trade with each other.

Dutch Settlers

By the 1600s, British and Dutch sailors had begun to take over control of the valuable Portuguese sea routes. They, too, landed at the Cape of Good Hope to trade pieces of metal and other trinkets for water and food. It became an important halfway stop for merchant ships on the long voyage between Europe and the Far East. Still, Table Bay was a dangerous place for ships, with the powerful winds and Atlantic waves driving many vessels to be wrecked on the coast.

In 1652, the powerful Dutch East India Company decided to make a permanent settlement at Table Bay, where ships could be repaired and sick men rested. They sent a young surgeon called Jan van Riebeeck with equipment and about one hundred

settlers. They built a mud-brick fort, which was soon replaced by a stone one, and began to cultivate the nearby land to grow fruit and vegetables. This area is still known as the Company's Gardens.

The Khoikhoi Are Forced Out

The Dutch needed a workforce to help look after these crops, but the Khoikhoi preferred to stay with their cattle herds. The Dutch East India Company brought in Muslims from Malaya and other parts of the Far East to work as slave laborers. Gradually, the Dutch settlement spread into the

▲ *Engraved in around 1675, this picture shows ships sailing into the harbor close to the Dutch settlement in today's Cape Town area.*

countryside, driving the Khoikhoi farther into the interior. In 1660, van Riebeeck even planted a hedge of bitter almond bushes from the foot of Table Mountain to the shore of Table Bay to mark the division between Europeans and native Africans.

As Dutch settlers seized more land, the Khoikhoi started to fight back. A series of bitter wars against the Khoikhoi ended in victory for the Dutch because of their guns

"This place looks prettier and more pleasant from the sea than it does when you are on land. It is rather miserable. There is no greenery or grass and the roads near the castle and the town's streets have holes and ruts, as if wild pigs had been rooting in them. . . . There is nothing pretty to be seen along the shoreline . . . the castle is very peculiar . . . the other houses here resemble prisons, and outside the Hottentots [Khoisan-speaking people], ugly and stinking people, and the houses of the Dutch are rather filthy too, and one sees here all sorts of peculiar people who live in strange ways."

—Johanna, granddaughter of Jan van Riebeeck, on a visit to the Dutch settlement in 1710.

and horses. By about 1680, both the Khoikhoi and the San peoples had lost their traditional lands, and weapons and diseases brought by the Europeans killed hundreds. They had little choice but to work as slave labor for the Dutch.

By 1750, the settlement had grown into a busy community with a population of more than three thousand and was called Kaapstad, which is Dutch for "Cape Town." It was adorned with many grand houses in the Cape Dutch style—symmetrical in design with ornamental curved gables—and was surrounded by thriving farms, vineyards, and gardens. Kaapstad was so popular with thirsty sailors from all over the world that it was known as "the Tavern of the Seas."

A British Colony

However, Dutch sea power was fading. In 1781, the French established a garrison to help the Dutch defend the city against British attack, but in 1795, a small British fleet arrived in Table Bay, anxious to grab control of the port before their French rivals did. The British easily forced the Dutch garrison to surrender but could not keep the port in their hands for long; it returned to Dutch control in 1803. The British retook the port three years later. In 1814, it became a colony of the growing British Empire. Trade expanded quickly, and many big European companies opened offices there.

The British were firmly in control, but they brought a greater freedom to the Cape than the Dutch had allowed. They abolished slavery in 1834 and let people follow any religion they liked. The Khoikhoi and San (who had now intermingled as the Khoisan) were given the protection of the law and allowed to own land. The remaining Dutch settlers (now known as Afrikaners) hated this liberal attitude. Most of them left the town and moved farther east into the interior of southern Africa.

Improving Communications

By the 1850s, Cape Town was growing fast, and it was becoming easier to reach the outside world. There were regular mail and passenger services by sea to Great Britain. A new road linked the city to Camps Bay, located west of Table Mountain. In 1860, a telegraph line was laid between Cape Town and Simon's Town, which had become a base for naval ships as well as whaling boats. There was even a railway running the short distance between the city and Wynberg to the south.

The most important work of this time was the building of two breakwaters, or long stone piers, which provided anchorage for ships safe from the violent seas of Table Bay. Each breakwater protected a dock—one named after Queen Victoria and the other after her son, Prince Alfred.

Meanwhile, two other events affected Cape Town's future. One was the discovery of rich deposits of gold and diamonds near present-day Johannesburg and Kimberley in South Africa. This brought a flood of miners and other immigrants from Europe, who landed at Cape Town on their way to the interior. The other event was the opening of the Suez Canal in Egypt in 1869, which created a shortcut from the Mediterranean to the Red Sea. Many ships could now avoid the long Cape journey altogether.

Cape Town Becomes a Capital

Between 1899 and 1902, the British fought the Boers (Dutch) to gain control of their

▲ By 1816, the year when this picture was painted, Cape Town was a British colony. A thriving community with many fine buildings, it was the capital of the Cape Colony.

territories in southern Africa. This Anglo-Boer War ended in British victory. The Union of South Africa was established in 1910, joining the separate provinces into one country, which governed itself but remained part of the British Empire. Cape Town had little to do with the war, but in 1910 became the new country's legislative capital.

White power was now stronger than ever in the Cape. The population of black Africans was growing fast, however, as hundreds came from country areas to find jobs. The new South African Parliament

Cecil Rhodes

Born in 1853 in Great Britain, Cecil Rhodes was a controversial figure in the growth of South Africa as a country. He came to Africa as a young man and made a fortune in the diamond mines. He then used his money to extend British power in the region, opposing other imperialist countries such as Belgium and Germany. In 1890, he became prime minister of the Cape Colony but was forced to resign in 1896 for his support of a campaign to overthrow the Boer-run government of the Transvaal. In 1902, he died at his cottage in Muizenberg, a small seaside town outside of Cape Town. The house is now the Rhodes' Cottage Museum, and a grand Rhodes Memorial, complete with bronze lions and a temple, (pictured here) can be seen near the Cape Town suburb of Rondebosch.

passed several laws that took away many of the rights of blacks and Cape Coloureds. It became harder for them to buy property, and in 1923, the Urban Areas Act forced them to live within specific parts the city. In 1936, Parliament even took away black people's right to vote in elections.

The Apartheid Years

Grimmer times lay ahead, however. In 1948, the right-wing National Party came to power in South Africa. This new government was even more determined to protect the wealth and lives of the white minority

13

▲ *Under apartheid, the system of racial segregation that existed in South Africa from 1948 to 1990, different races were not allowed to use the same amenities. As this picture shows, beaches were racially segregated, with the best often reserved for whites.*

against competition from the black majority. It began to build the system known as apartheid—the separation, or segregation, of the racial groups. South Africa's laws treated whites, blacks, and Cape Coloureds quite differently.

Black people suffered the most. They had to carry identification papers wherever they went, and they were forbidden to own most businesses. In the Cape Town area, they were forbidden to take certain jobs if a Cape Coloured person was available instead. Men from country districts trying to work in the city were not allowed to bring their families to live with them. Families were separated for years at a time.

The most hated apartheid law was the Group Areas Act of 1966, which forced black people out of the towns and into the desolate townships that sprang up in places such as Cape Flats, southeast of Cape Town. District Six, a vibrant and racially mixed community near downtown, was declared to be a whites-only area. More than fifty thousand blacks and Cape Coloureds were evicted, and bulldozers smashed down the buildings. No whites went to live there, however; it remained a wasteland for many years.

Resistance and Freedom

There were many acts of protest against the apartheid laws. Organizations such as the African National Congress (ANC) led the resistance with strikes, peaceful demonstrations, and mass meetings. The government responded savagely. ANC leaders were arrested and many of them, including Nelson Mandela, were imprisoned for many years on Robben Island in Table Bay.

Despite the arrests, the anti-apartheid movement kept growing. In 1983, more than fifteen thousand people came to Mitchell's Plain on Cape Flats to form the United Democratic Front (UDF) as an even bigger opposition force than the ANC.

Robben Island

Robben Island, 8 miles (13 km) off Green Point, was originally a base for whaling ships. Starting in about 1810, however, it became a prison island, from which no one could possibly escape. Between 1960 and 1991, it was used to house political prisoners, many of them heroic figures in South Africa's struggle for liberation from apartheid. The most famous were Nelson Mandela and Walter Sisulu, who spent twenty-five years there.

Other countries supported the movement by refusing to trade with South Africa, creating an economic crisis in Cape Town as fewer cargo ships came to the docks.

The white government remained determined to make the city's downtown area a whites-only zone. Between May and June of 1986, they drove an estimated seventy thousand people from their homes in Cape Town. Hundreds were killed, prompting an international outcry. Because of foreign governments' intense pressure on

Nelson Mandela

Nelson Mandela was born in 1918 in Transkei, eastern South Africa. His father was a tribal chief, but the young Mandela did not want a traditional life. He trained as one of the country's first black lawyers and became involved in politics, especially the movement against apartheid. His political activities led to a life sentence in jail in 1964 for treason and sabotage, and he spent most of the next twenty-six years as a prisoner on Robben Island. After a worldwide campaign, he was released in 1990 and became South Africa's first black president in 1994. Mandela retired from the presidency in 1999 and from public life in 2004. The picture above shows Mandela (center) at his inauguration ceremony flanked by his deputies: ex-president F.W. de Klerk (left) and current president, Thabo Mbeki (right).

the South African government and the resistance movement's work, conditions started to improve in the late 1980s.

New Government, New Goals

The white-dominated government could not suppress black South Africans forever. Student demonstrations erupted across the country when, among other things, the government ruled that Afrikaans had to be used as the sole language of instruction in nonwhite schools. Police action against peaceful protests led to increasingly large and violent anti-apartheid demonstrations across the country throughout the 1980s. In 1986, Desmond Tutu became the country's first black archbishop at St. George's

Cathedral in Cape Town. He strongly advocated continuing peaceful protests against apartheid and for a change in government to represent all the peoples of South Africa.

In December 1989, South Africa's President F. W. de Klerk secretly negotiated with Nelson Mandela for his release from prison. Mandela refused to be freed unless the white president would agree to work toward a constitution that would give equal rights and the vote to all South Africans. Cape Town's City Hall became the setting for the first public speech by Nelson Mandela after he was released from prison in 1990. Apartheid collapsed, and in 1994, Mandela became the first black president of South Africa.

The new government had two major goals—to create better housing and other social conditions and to reconcile the bitter divisions between blacks and whites. The development program has been agonizingly slow, even though cities such as Cape Town are building thousands of new homes every year. The healing of old wounds, however, has been very successful, thanks to the work of the Truth and Reconciliation Commission, which has been exploring the human-rights abuses and crimes of the apartheid era.

The ANC won another resounding victory in the general election of 1999, after which Nelson Mandela stepped down, and Thabo Mbeki became the new president. South Africa's third election, in April 2004,

▲ *Thabo Mbeki succeeded Nelson Mandela in 1997 as president of the African National Congress, then in 1999 as president of the Republic of South Africa. He was reelected to office in April 2004.*

resulted in the ANC gaining an even greater share of the vote—more than two-thirds. Mbeki promised to improve roads, railway links, and other parts of the infrastructure and to create at least one million new jobs. He also vowed to give back land to those black and mixed-race people deprived of property during the apartheid era.

CHAPTER 2

People of Cape Town

The population of Cape Town is unlike any other in South Africa. For a start, it has a unique mixture of races and cultures that originally arrived from Europe and Asia as well as many parts of Africa. Although black Africans are by far the biggest group in the country as a whole, they make up just over 30 percent of Cape Town's population. Cape Coloured people are one of the smaller ethnic groups in South Africa, but here they make up almost half the total.

The Cape Coloured Community

Three main elements have gone into the racial makeup of the Cape Coloureds. From the time of the Dutch arrival in the seventeenth century, Europeans and the local Khoikhoi mingled and married to produce children of mixed race. Later, the Dutch brought in slaves from India, the Malay Peninsula, and other parts of the Far East; many of these also married Europeans. The descendants of these peoples form the huge Cape Coloured population today.

It is not a separate and distinct community. Once used by the ruling whites to define

◀ *Mostly Cape Coloured people participate in the annual Cape Town Minstrel Carnival, a traditional month-long event that first began in 1834 to celebrate the end of slavery.*

people who were not black Africans or white, today the term has less meaning because "Coloured" people cover a huge range of skin shades, from nearly white to nearly black. The vast majority of Cape Coloureds have the same kinds of lifestyle, jobs, and aspirations as other racial groups in the city.

Most of them follow the Protestant branch of the Christian faith. Many descendants of the Cape Malays (so called because Malay was their common language), however, have kept the Muslim religion of their old homelands in various parts of Southeast Asia. The traditional Cape Malay, or Cape Muslim, quarter of the city is the Bo-Kaap on the eastern side of Signal Hill, and many still live there.

The Black Community

Nobody knows exactly how many black people live in Cape Town. The sprawling townships of the Cape Flats have a huge black population that is always changing and impossible to count accurately. Other big township areas in Atlantis and Philadelphia sprawl north of the city. The more well-paid black people can afford to live in the city's center and the wealthier suburbs.

Even so, blacks make up only about one-third of the city's total population. Most of them are descendants of the Xhosa people. Many thousands have migrated to Cape Town in recent years from the Xhosa "homelands" in the east, where they were forced to live during the apartheid years.

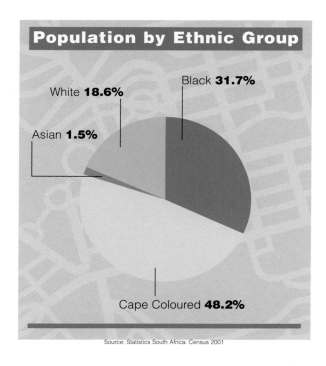

Population by Ethnic Group

White **18.6%**

Black **31.7%**

Asian **1.5%**

Cape Coloured **48.2%**

Source: Statistics South Africa: Census 2001

There are also numbers of people from other southern African groups, including the Zulu and the Ndebele.

The White Community

White people make up about 18 percent of Cape Town's population—a far larger proportion than in other South African cities. This is probably because the land now called Western Cape Province was one of the first areas in southern Africa where Europeans settled and pushed out the native Africans. It remained a white stronghold until the end of the apartheid era in 1994.

There are two main white groups. One group is descended from the original Dutch settlers and mainly speaks Afrikaans. The other is descended from the later British settlers and primarily speaks English.

Cape Town Lingo

Here are a few words and phrases used by Cape people. They are a mixture of Dutch, Afrikaans, English, and Xhosa.

Cape Town Word	Pronunciation	Meaning
asseblief	ahs-suh-bleef	please
bergie	behrr-hee	a homeless person
dankie	dahn-kee	thank you
goeie more	ghoo-yeh more-ah	good morning
gogga	ghoe-gghah	bug or insect
ja	yah	yes
larney	lahr-nee	cool, fashionable
skollie	skawl-lee	township gangster
tackies	tak-kees	athletic shoes
twak	twahk	nonsense

There are some much smaller groups of whites from other parts of Europe, including Portugal and Hungary.

Many Languages in One City

You can hear at least a dozen different languages or local dialects on the Cape Town streets, and there are eleven official languages—not surprising when you think of the great variety of ethnic backgrounds in the population. One of the most common is Afrikaans, which developed from the Dutch language of the early settlers. It is a simpler version than the original Dutch, with many words borrowed from African languages as well as a sprinkling of English, French, and Malay terms. Most Capetonians can speak Afrikaans, especially the Cape Coloured and white citizens.

The other widely used language is English. South African English has developed a flavor of its own over the centuries, however, and features many words borrowed from other languages. South Africans usually speak it with the hard, flat local accent, which even some British visitors find hard to understand.

Most black people in big cities such as Cape Town use either English or Afrikaans as a common language when they need to. At home, however, they are likely to speak one of the African languages; there are at least ten of these native to southern Africa, each with several different dialects, or versions. The most popular in Cape Town is Xhosa, the tongue of the peoples who settled here fifteen hundred years ago. Like English and Afrikaans, Xhosa has picked up many outside influences along the way, notably several click sounds originally used by the Khoikhoi.

"We are the rainbow people! We are the new people of South Africa!"

—Archbishop Desmond Tutu in 1989 after leading thirty thousand anti-apartheid demonstrators from St. George's Cathedral to City Hall.

Desmond Tutu

Born in Transvaal in 1931, Desmond Tutu (pictured here with Nelson Mandela on the right) *trained as a teacher and then as an Anglican priest. He became the first black senior priest of Johannesburg in 1975. Energetic and charming, Tutu was soon a leading critic of the apartheid system, although he argued against the use of violence against the government. In 1984, he won the Nobel Peace Prize for his work and two years later was appointed as the first black archbishop of Cape Town. After the apartheid era ended, Tutu became the chairman of the Truth and Reconciliation Commission. His honesty and fairness have done much to help heal South Africa's racial divisions.*

Christians

Followers of all the major world religions live in Cape Town. By far the largest group, about 90 percent, are the Christians, as they are in other parts of South Africa. They belong to many very different branches of the Christian faith. The traditional faith of the white European minority is the Dutch Reformed Church; its "mother church" is the Groote Kerk on Adderley Street. This church was first built on this site in 1704; parts of the original remain in the building constructed between 1836 and 1841. It boasts a beautiful carved pulpit.

Dozens of independent black Christian churches also flourish, many founded by the black Africans themselves because they did not agree with some of the teachings of the white Christian missionaries in the nineteenth and twentieth centuries. Followers of these churches often wear special clothing decorated with crosses or stars to the services.

British settlers brought their Church of England religious practices with them. Built in the early twentieth century, the Church of England cathedral is St. George's in Wale Street. Today, the Church of England's most famous member is Desmond Tutu. He became Archbishop of Cape Town in 1986 and was a national hero and leader in the struggle against apartheid.

Islam and Other Religions

Cape Town is an important center for Muslims in South Africa; they make up about 6 percent of the city's population. More than ten thousand Muslims still live in the Bo-Kaap area of the City Bowl, which contains an Islamic museum called the

Bo-Kaap Museum, as well as the distinctive minarets of no fewer than eleven mosques. These include the Auwal on Dorp Street, South Africa's first official mosque, which was founded in the 1790s.

There are also sizeable groups of Hindus and people of other religions in the city. Some blacks follow the traditional African religions, which are often combined with elements of Western Christianity and other faiths. More than fifteen thousand Jews live in Cape Town, most of them descended from refugees who fled here from Eastern Europe in the nineteenth and twentieth centuries. The Great Synagogue, with its dome and twin towers, stands next to the Jewish Museum on Hatfield Street.

▼ Cape Town Muslims crowd into the mosques for special prayers during the major celebrations. If the mosques are full, people pray outside on the street.

Food and Cooking

Cape Town's food reflects the rich mix of its population. People like to go out to restaurants to eat, and there is probably a wider range of restaurants here than in any other South African city. The City Bowl, especially the Victoria and Alfred Waterfront, contains restaurants that specialize in the usual international fare—everything from Italian pizzas and American burgers to Thai dishes and Indian curries.

Much more exciting are the local cooking styles developed over the centuries. Traditional Cape cuisine combines influences brought by the Dutch and by Malay slaves from Indonesia as well as other parts of Asia. The result is spicy and unusual. Famous Cape dishes include *bredies*, which are stews of lamb or mutton with quince, pumpkin, or special water flowers and *bobotie*, which is chopped meat with

dried fruit and spices covered with unsweetened custard.

Seafood from the waters around the Cape is a vital element in cooking. A codlike fish called *snoek* is a special favorite of Capetonians, who like it in their

▲ *Cape Town has many restaurants and cafés that offer a wide range of international cuisines, particularly within the City Bowl.*

Exotic Eating

Although beef is very popular as well as chicken, mutton, and pork, there is also a growing demand for the meat of more exotic animals such as antelope, ostriches, and even warthogs. Some local farmers have begun breeding these animals so that they can supply the city markets. Beef is the basis for biltong, *the famous Afrikaaner version of meat dried in the sun and wind. The equivalent for black Africans is dried* mopane, *the caterpillar that feeds on the mopane tree.*

sandwiches. It is caught on the Atlantic side of the Cape in the winter months and served fresh or preserved by being smoked or salted. Clams, oysters, and other shellfish come from the warmer Indian Ocean on the eastern side of the peninsula.

At home, the most popular kind of summer meal is a barbecue, or *braai*. South Africans love meat of all kinds (ranging from beef to antelope), especially when it is grilled over an open fire. People in the poorer districts, especially the Cape Flats townships, can rarely afford this sort of food. Their staple diet is usually a cheap and fatty meat stew served with corn porridge called *pap*.

CHAPTER 3

Living in Cape Town

Cape Town has been a magnet for all kinds of people throughout its long history. Today, the population of the metropolitan area is growing at a faster rate than ever before, largely due to the steady arrival of thousands of black Africans migrating to the townships from poorer rural districts.

Housing in the City's Center

The City Bowl is really an area of offices, shops, markets, hotels, many historical buildings, and museums. Housing space is very limited, and only the wealthy can afford to live here or in the old inner-city suburbs nearby such as Gardens or Tamboerskloof. Even more exclusive are Clifton and Camps Bay, set above the beautiful beaches on the Atlantic shore west of Table Mountain.

Most of the Cape Coloured and black populations were forcibly moved out of the city center during the apartheid era, and few have ever returned. There are still districts such as the Bo-Kaap, however, where the traditional communities have survived.

◀ *In the center of downtown and surrounded by attractive buildings, Greenmarket Square has a lively outdoor market filled with stalls selling crafts and clothing.*

Many residents here descend from the slaves brought here from Southeast Asia by the Dutch. Most of these people follow the Sufi religion, which is a part of the Islamic faith, and speak their own version of Afrikaans. These days, the charm of the steep cobbled streets and brightly painted cube-shaped houses is making the Bo-Kaap a fashionable area for rich whites to live.

The Suburbs

Most whites and Cape Coloureds have their homes in the sprawling Southern Suburbs, from where they can travel to work in the city. In the last one hundred years, the suburbs have been built outward in successive waves to house the growing middle-class population. Now they stretch east of Table Mountain and south from the city toward False Bay.

Each part of the suburbs has its own special atmosphere. Woodstock, nearest the center, is an old, established area with

Groot Constantia

Perhaps the greatest of all Cape Town's houses is Groot Constantia in the oldest and most exclusive part of the Southern Suburbs. Tucked into the side of Table Mountain, it is the manor house of a winery estate first established by a Dutch governor in 1685. With its whitewashed walls, ornate roof gables, and delicate stone carvings, it is an important example of Cape Dutch architecture.

run-down housing that is slowly being fixed up. Observatory and Rosebank, next to it, are cheerful and scruffy districts where many students from the University of Cape Town are housed. Further south still are Newlands and Claremont, the most elegant suburbs where houses are very expensive. With their own shopping malls, markets, and movie complexes, they offer people an alternative to living in the city's center.

The Township Housing Crisis

The black and Cape Coloured townships of Cape Flats lie just east of the suburbs. They are a stark contrast to the suburbs because they are primarily camps where migrant workers have built patchwork shelters on empty land. The houses are made of any material available—wood, corrugated iron, plastic sheets, and even old containers from cargo ships. Three families sometimes share a single room. There is no proper sewage system or running water, and chickens, goats, and sheep wander the streets. In such cramped and poverty-stricken conditions, disease and crime flourish.

Since apartheid ended, thousands of people have come to Cape Town to look for

▲ *Guguletu township, about 9 miles (14 km)
outside the city, is a mixture of informal shanty
homes and brick housing.*

work. As a result, the populations in the townships and squatter camps have soared. In 1993, more than 24,000 families lived in Cape Flats. By 2004, the figure had risen to 100,000 families. Despite the government's house-building program, the number of homeless people is still going up. Each year, about 10,000 new homes are completed, but that still leaves 250,000 people to find houses for.

In August 2001, torrential rain caused flooding on Cape Flats. The rains drained off the higher ground and turned the treeless dusty area of the Flats into a sea of mud and water. Hundreds of families were forced to flee the shantytowns as their weak and patched-up homes were damaged. The deep water took a long time to drain away because there was no proper sewage system. This, and the lack of freshwater to drink, brought a threat of disease.

A vibrant and creative community has grown up in the middle of this hardship, however. There is a strong African tradition of warm hospitality, and the city government and local businesses are trying to attract tourists to stay in township homes and meet the locals. The *shebeens* (unlicensed drinking clubs) are the home of township jazz, an exciting mixture of African rhythms and American jazz, which also draw tourists.

Since the black majority took power in South Africa, large areas of these shantytowns have been bulldozed. In their place, the Cape Town government has built estates of simple four-roomed houses, with running water, flush toilets, and electricity. These are known as "Mandela" houses after the country's first postapartheid president, and township dwellers are given government grants to help buy them.

Stores and Markets

Most Capetonians buy their goods in American-style malls where they can find almost every kind of store. These malls include the Gardens Centre in Mill Street, the giant Cavendish Square in Claremont,

▶ *The hugely popular Victoria and Alfred Waterfront complex offers luxury goods in an American-style mall environment as well as a variety of markets selling local crafts.*

and the even bigger Victoria and Alfred Waterfront, which has everything from supermarkets to craft markets. There are also several lively traditional markets that open through the week, such as the ones at Cape Town Station and Grand Parade. The streets of the Bo-Kaap are lined with spice stalls.

Starting up a store in the townships is difficult because few people have cash to buy goods to sell in the first place. Local residents often band together, however, to loan individuals enough money so that simple stalls called *spaza* shops can be established. These manage to survive by selling a few cheap goods and by staying open for long hours.

Growing Up

Cape Town is an exciting place to grow up in. Its warm climate means that children can spend much of their time outdoors, enjoying the many parks and the wide

"I'm going to be thanking the government because we have a house now. Then maybe I'll ask God if he can help us with jobs."

—Alpha Lupuzi, resident of Cape Flats, 2004.

▲ *After Nelson Mandela's government ended apartheid in 1994, racially segregated schools were abolished, but there is still little racial mixing in the majority of South Africa's schools.*

beaches that surround the city. Even more important is the feeling of hope for the future among young people. For the first time in Cape Town's history, children of all races are growing up together with equal rights and opportunities.

On the other hand, life for children in the black townships can still be very hard.

Even if their family has a new Mandela home, they are often poor because jobs are hard to find. Children have to share one of the two small bedrooms and rarely have enough food to eat. One mother told a local radio station in 2003 that her daughters are sometimes so hungry that they cry.

Education

Legally, all children have to attend school beginning at the age of seven, although many schools enroll six-year olds. They start at primary school, going on to junior

The Cost of Schooling

The fees families must pay to have their children attend school vary hugely in Cape Town, depending on the area where they live. A township school, often lacking most equipment and facilities, can charge as little as $4 a year. A state-run school in the suburbs will cost at least $40 a year—ten times as much. Most expensive are the well-equipped private schools, which may charge pupils at least $240 a year and can reach over $5,000 annually. Although South Africa now has no official racial segregation, the more expensive schools are usually confined to whites and Cape Coloureds since few blacks can afford the costs.

secondary school at twelve. At age fifteen, students take exams for their General Certificate to graduate and can leave school if they want. Many go on to senior secondary school or to a technical school where they are taught practical skills.

Under apartheid, education was run on racial lines, which meant that white children had the best schooling, and about one-quarter of the black children never

"Parents still see across racial lines. There's a stigma associated with being a coloured school."

—Anthony Hess, Head of Groenberg High School.

went to school at all. Since 1994, schools have officially been open to everyone. Government spending on black education has increased enormously; in the last ten years, the number of pupils at primary schools has shot up nationwide from two million to nearly eight million.

Despite these changes, the education system is still a very unequal one. Former white schools still have all the best equipment and facilities (and still primarily serve white students), while most black schools struggle to keep going. Ummangaliso Primary School In Khayelitsha, for example, has fourteen hundred black pupils and just two computers. Many of these children depend on the school for their main meal of the day—two slices of bread and a milkshake. Burglars have stolen nearly everything from the building, even the toilet bowls.

At the age of eighteen, pupils take a test for their Senior Certificate. If they pass, they may choose to go on to higher education, though the majority of parents cannot afford to pay the college fees. The University of Cape Town in Rondebosch is one of South Africa's major universities, but most of its students are white. The University of Western Cape in nearby Bellville attracts mainly Cape Coloureds. Cape Town also has several other colleges, including technikons where students learn technical subjects such as information technology, electronics, mechanical engineering, and building-construction skills.

CHAPTER 4

Cape Town at Work

Cape Town has always been a prosperous place, especially in the nineteenth century. Today, its wealth and population are growing more rapidly than ever before. Since the end of apartheid, the national government has encouraged foreign companies to invest in South Africa, and Cape Town has benefited hugely. Business has boomed in many areas such as tourism and new kinds of manufacturing, and there has been a steady increase in the city's oldest trade—the export of goods by sea.

Big Business

Financial and business services form an important slice of Cape Town's economy. Many of the country's major finance companies have their headquarters here. These include insurers such as Old Mutual, finance houses such as Merrill Lynch that offer and service loans to businesses, and merchant and capital banks such as First National and New Republic. Multinational oil companies also have a strong presence, notably Shell, Caltex, and BP.

The main business districts are in the downtown area—especially the rapidly

◄ *The fishing harbor at Hout Bay is the center of the crayfish and snoek fishing industry. Fish are one of Cape Town's top exports.*

▲ *Cape Town's Groot Constantia is one of the oldest wine estates in South Africa. Cape Province is a major wine-producing area internationally.*

Pollution and the Environment

Like all big cities, Cape Town has major pollution problems. The population is getting bigger and buying more, and this has led to a huge jump in the volume of waste. The growth of industry and the increase in car use causes air pollution, which sometimes forms a brown haze that hangs over the city. The lack of proper sewage systems in areas such as Cape Flats means that wastewater runs straight into the sea, polluting the coastal waters. In 2001, the City of Cape Town introduced a strict program to monitor and counter these threats to its environment.

growing Victoria and Alfred Waterfront—and Claremont. There are also several large business parks in Blackheath, Tygerberg, and other outer suburbs and a brand new Cape Town International Conference Centre on Coen Steytler Avenue.

Industry

Many Capetonians (over 9 percent of the workforce) have jobs in factories and workshops. A few of these are large companies producing heavy goods such as steel, machinery, and motor vehicles. The vast majority, however, are much smaller and employ fewer than fifty workers. They produce a huge variety of articles, from artificial fibers and clothing to shoes and hand tools.

Cape Town's food industry provides work for just as many people, including

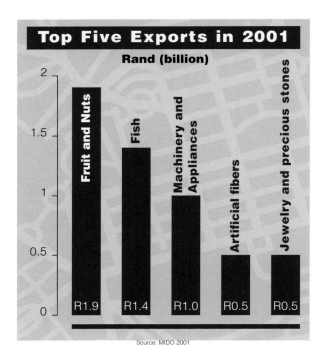

Top Five Exports in 2001
Rand (billion)

Fruit and Nuts	R1.9
Fish	R1.4
Machinery and Appliances	R1.0
Artificial fibers	R0.5
Jewelry and precious stones	R0.5

Source: MIDO 2001

▲ This chart shows Cape Town's top five export categories in rands (billion), South Africa's currency. These products make up 46 percent of Cape Town's total exports for the year 2001.

processing fruit, fish, and other local foods. The most famous product of the Western Cape area, however, is its wine. There are over 150 vineyards to the south and east of the city; the biggest and oldest of them is Groot Constantia, with its grand homestead near Kirstenbosch Botanical Gardens. Large teams of temporary workers pick the grapes at harvest time.

Tourism and the Media

More than 7.5 million visitors come to Cape Town every year, both from abroad and from other parts of South Africa. The city has thousands of hotels, bed-and-breakfasts, and backpackers' hostels to cater to this flood of people, as well as restaurants and shops. Many residents make their living from the tourist industry, including street traders and organizers of tours around and outside the city. Escorted visits to the townships are becoming very popular.

Cape Town also lures crowds for another reason—as a favorite location for international crews making commercials or feature films. They like the fine weather, dramatic settings, and the fact that films are cheaper to produce here. A whole new industry has grown up in the city to support filmmakers, including agencies to supply actors and technical companies dealing with everything from scenery and lighting to equipment repairs. A massive new film studio, the biggest in Africa, opened in the Southern Suburbs in 2005, creating new jobs for up to eight thousand people.

The city is also a major media center. More than forty national magazines are printed here as well as the four local newspapers—the *Cape Times*, *City Vision*, and *Cape Argus* in English and the Afrikaans-language *Die Burger*. There are three radio stations mixing music and talk, including Radio 786 Online, which caters especially to the city's Muslim population.

Employment and Wages

Cape Town is richer and more successful than most other areas in South Africa, and its workforce is more highly skilled and literate (able to read and write). Even so, it is hard for many people to find a job. Figures show that more than 20 percent of the population was unemployed in 2002, and the figure is rising. Blacks and Cape Coloureds often suffer worst. They were excluded from most kinds of employment during the apartheid era and, therefore, must struggle to gain competitive skills and experience in the job market.

A shortage of jobs means that wages in the region are often very low. About one-fourth of all workers earn less than 1,000 rand ($152 at 2004 rates) per month in a country where a loaf of bread costs about 3.7 rand (57¢). The largest group of workers, about 40 percent, make between 1,000 and 2,000 rand ($152 and $306) per month. A black maid working for a white family can earn as little as 150 rand ($23) a month, while many vineyard workers are paid even less—120 rand ($18) a month. Builders and factory workers receive an average of about 2,800 rand ($427) a month, but even this is at the bottom end of the pay scale. Workers in the financial or service industries earn nearly three times as much.

Government

In 2000, six local city governments joined together to form the Cape Town Council,

▼ *South Africa's Houses of Parliament are located in Cape Town. In this picture, members of Parliament have gathered to hear President Mbeki speak during the official opening of Parliament in 2004.*

or city government. The new council governs the whole metropolitan area under the leadership of a mayor. The people of the city elect the two hundred council members (two for each ward or area) using a voting system based on proportional representation.

The council is in overall charge of the departments that control every aspect of city affairs. These include town planning, health, the environment, finance, tourism, and housing as well as daily services such as public transportation and waste disposal.

Cape Town also plays a major role in the national government of South Africa. It is the country's legislative capital and home of the grand, nineteenth-century Houses of Parliament, where laws are discussed, altered, and passed. South Africa is a democracy, in which every adult can vote to elect members to the Parliament. Since 1994, this has been made up of two separate Chambers, or Houses—the National Assembly with four hundred members elected by the people and the Senate with ninety members elected by provincial (local) assemblies.

Law and Order

Crime is a major problem in the city, especially in the townships where, in some areas, the murder rate is one of the highest in the world. Since apartheid ended, muggings, robberies, and other violent crimes have actually increased at the same time as the gulf has grown between rich and poor people.

The police have made huge efforts in

Violent Crime

In 2002, more than 24,000 people died in Cape Town. Of these, 2,290 were classed as "violent" deaths, caused by stabbings or shootings. Khayelitsha township in Cape Flats tops every other area in South Africa for the number of murders committed each year— 47.4 murders for every 100,000 people, eight times the average in the United States.

recent years to curb this crime epidemic. They have installed a closed-circuit television system to cover the central city and inner suburbs. More than three hundred community patrol officers have been recruited to work with regular officers in controlling traffic and dealing with street crime. A special police unit helps tourists who get into difficulties.

Moving around Cape Town

As Cape Town has become bigger and more prosperous, its traffic has increased. It has a good road system, however, with several stretches of modern freeway that allow vehicles to travel in and out of downtown. The morning and evening rush hours are usually the only times when major traffic jams occur. As in other parts of South Africa, drivers are often careless and ignore speed restrictions so accidents are common.

The main city bus terminals are in Adderley Street and near the Golden Acre shopping center. Bus services are geared for

▲ *The world-famous Blue Train runs between Pretoria and Cape Town just three times each week, allowing wealthy passengers to enjoy the scenery in luxury.*

Duncan Dock

A series of docks, the Victoria and Alfred Basins were begun in the nineteenth century. By the 1930s, it was obvious that they were too small to deal with the bigger and bigger cargo ships arriving in port so, in 1938, work started on a new dock just to the east. Duncan Dock, as it was named, covered a large part of the old waterfront of Woodstock and Paarden Island. Today, this is Cape Town's major working dock area, with harbors, cranes, and other facilities able to handle even the largest supertankers.

workers commuting in and out of the town, so most buses only run between 6:30 A.M. and 6:30 P.M. Many people prefer to use the minibus taxis (or combi-taxis) that are operated by private companies. These hold up to fifteen passengers (sometimes even more) and are usually driven at terrifying speed, but they are cheap and cover most areas of the city.

The local train system is called the Metro, but few local trains run after 6 P.M. on weekdays either. The railroad carries passengers from Cape Town's central station south and east to Simon's Town, Strand, and Stellenbosch. There are also long-distance services to other major South African cities. Cape Town's busy International Airport is 14 miles (22 km) east of the city on Cape Flats.

CHAPTER 5

Cape Town at Play

The people of Cape Town take great pleasure in their time off from work. This is hardly surprising in a city with such wonderful natural gifts—a warm but not scorching climate, beautiful sea and landscape all around, and a generally relaxed attitude to life. Sports are a national obsession in South Africa, and if Capetonians are not playing a sport (anything from tennis or golf to riding horses, surfing, or cycling), then they are watching one.

The Great Outdoors

Most free time is spent outside, and there is an enormous choice of recreational activities. Many people head for the vast stretches of beach that almost surround Cape Town, though the waters on the Atlantic (west) coast are usually too cold for swimmers without wet suits. The favorite spots for surfing, windsurfing, or scuba diving are on the False Bay side, especially at Llandudno, Muizenberg, and Noordhoek.

Cape Town is right next to the Cape Peninsula National Park, an area of mountains, woods, and scrub-covered hills.

◄ *Warm waters that are safe for swimming and a long, sandy beach have made Muizenberg a popular resort. Rows of brightly colored cabins (for changing into swimsuits) line the beachfront.*

The park provides the perfect setting for a number of outdoor sports including hiking, rappeling, hang gliding, and bungee jumping. The Cape of Good Hope Nature Reserve, Kommetjie (a tidal pool and surfing spot), and Hout Bay (a cove with a beautiful beach) attract many naturalists

▲ *Table Mountain offers recreational opportunities for those who dare; here, people rappel from the top of the mountain against the backdrop of Lion's Head.*

who come to watch eland, rhebok (a kind of antelope), and other animals—as well as to watch out for the dangerous cobras and venomous puff adders.

Cape Town's biggest park is, of course, Table Mountain itself. This looming, flat-topped peak with its gorges and cliffs is right in the middle of the city and is a favorite weekend destination for locals. There are dozens of walks and climbs to the summit, not to mention more than fourteen hundred kinds of flowers, baboons, and "dassies," or hyraxes, which are rabbit-sized mammals with hooves. Less energetic people take the cable car to the top from Kloof Nek Road.

Kloofing

One of the toughest outdoor pastimes on the Western Cape is kloofing. *A kloof is a cliff or gorge, and* kloofers *explore such places, usually following a mountain river from its source. This activity can involve climbing, wading, hopping from rock to rock, and even swimming down stream. Kloofers need to know the area—and its pitfalls—to avoid getting into problems.*

Watching the Whales

One of the most spectacular natural sights of the Cape Peninsula is the arrival of the whales. Between August and November, many species of whale come to breed in the sheltered waters east of Cape Town. Mother whales and their calves can be seen swimming and playing from many points near the city, especially above Muizenberg and from the Simon's Town beaches.

Sport Fans

Cape Town is one of the country's major sports centers. The two most popular games are cricket and rugby football. Huge crowds always fill the fine cricket ground at Newlands for provincial and international matches. The nearby Newlands Rugby Stadium is home ground for the Western Province and Western Cape teams and a venue for international games against touring teams.

Rugby, however, is still seen largely as a sport for whites. Soccer is quickly catching up in popularity, especially among the blacks and Cape Coloureds of the townships. South Africa's first-ever appearance in the World Cup Finals in 1996 boosted their enthusiasm. The most famous soccer player from the city is Quinton Fortune, who grew up in Cape Flats and now plays for England's famous Manchester United team.

Night Life

Many Capetonians spend their evenings visiting the huge number of clubs, bars, and other entertainment centers. The main areas for nightclubs in the City Bowl are the Victoria and Alfred Waterfront and Long Street, but perhaps the most lively music scene is in the Cape Flats townships.

During the apartheid era, Cape Town theaters staged several protest plays, including works by the world-famous playwright Athol Fugard. Many of these venues survive today, although the plays are now more likely to be operas or musicals. South Africa's best-known comedian,

◄ *Capetonian cricket player Herschelle Gibbs is one of the world's top batsmen. He is seen here playing for South Africa at Newlands Cricket Ground in 2004.*

Pieter-Dirk Uys, began his career here. Movie theaters range from multiplexes like the Nu Metro and Imax on the Victoria and Alfred Waterfront to smaller independent houses like the Armchair Theatre in Observatory. Cape Town stages a film festival every April, including work by new and experimental filmmakers.

Museums and Festivals

Many aspects of Cape Town's varied history and culture are on display in the city's museums. Some contain great treasures, such as the precious artworks in the Gold of Africa Museum or the contemporary South African art in the South African National Gallery. Others recall grimmer passages of the racist past, including the Cape Town Holocaust Centre on Hatfield Street and the Nelson Mandela Gateway and Museum on Robben Island. The Two Oceans Aquarium on the Waterfront, with its sharks and other amazing exhibits, is one of the best aquariums in the world.

Like many other cities, Cape Town starts its year with the usual New Year celebrations, but then, on January 2, comes the *Tweedenuwejaar* or "Second New Year." This time of noisy celebrations centers on the Cape Minstrel Carnival at the Green Point stadium and features parades and singing and dancing contests between groups of minstrels (musicians) in painted faces, straw hats, and bright costumes.

Two sporting events are big moments in Cape Town's calendar. The Cape to Rio

Cape Town's Greatest Jazz Musician

Dollar Brand was born in 1934 in Kensington, then one of Cape Town's poorest Cape Coloured ghettos, and named Adolphus Brand. He was inspired to play piano by his grandmother, who was a pianist at the local church. Because of his race, he was barred from music school so he started performing jazz in bars and clubs at age fifteen. Soon Dollar Brand was famous for his brilliance and the African rhythms in his music. After mixed-race bands became illegal in 1976, he fled to the United States but returned when Nelson Mandela was released in 1990. Now a Muslim with the Islamic name of Abdullah Ibrahim, he has released more than one hundred albums.

Yacht Race is staged every two years in February. Sailing boats set out from the docks to race across the Atlantic to South America. The Two Oceans Marathon in April is run along the Atlantic and Indian Ocean sides of the Cape. One of the longest marathon runs in the world, it is actually one-and-a half marathon lengths—35 miles (56 km).

Many other celebrations through the year are connected with food and drink. For instance, the Stellenbosch Wine Festivals take place in March and October, the Snoek Festival at Hout Bay in June, and the Knysna Oyster Festival in July. There are also several music and art festivals.

CHAPTER 6

Looking Forward

Cape Town has more natural advantages than almost any other city in the world, allowing it to develop with growing speed since the end of the apartheid system in 1990. Along with Cairo, Egypt, it has become the joint number one tourist destination in Africa. This startling development has brought a mixture of old problems and new challenges.

Rich and Poor

Cape Town has always been a city of contrasts—governors and slaves, grand mansions and shantytowns, wealth and poverty. As it expands, many of these differences worsen. There is a bigger divide than ever between rich and poor, and the rich minority continue to have the easiest access to parks, beaches, and other natural open spaces. As tourism, road traffic, and industrial output have grown, so has pollution of the land, sea, and air.

The city council has identified these problems and begun to draw up plans to tackle them. They are designing new public spaces and looking for public and private money to help build them. This project is

◄ *A colony of penguins live at the popular Boulders Beach, close to Simon's Town, one of the area's many natural attractions that have made Cape Town a tourist magnet. As tourism increases, however, higher levels of pollution pose a greater threat to the environment.*

A Killer Disease in Cape Town

As in other parts of South Africa, the biggest danger to Cape Town's health is AIDS (Acquired Immune Deficiency Syndrome), which is caused by HIV (Human Immunodeficiency Virus). More than two thousand people died of it in the city during 2002, making it the city's biggest single killer. Effective drugs to combat AIDS are at long last becoming cheaply available. These, combined with a network of special AIDS clinics, are beginning to reduce the misery and deaths caused by the disease.

called the Uluntu Plaza program, from the Xhosa and dialect words meaning "gathering places for all." The council is also planning to improve public transportation, which is primarily used by the poor because they are least likely to

have cars, and is keeping a close watch on pollution levels.

Continuing Growth

Cape Town is remote from other large towns and especially far from South Africa's industrial heartland. There is plenty of opportunity for its own manufacturing sectors to grow, especially steelmaking, a vital supply industry for shipbuilding and other heavy construction sectors. It also has attractive living and working conditions in the downtown area and suburbs, which are drawing many new industries to the area, such as information technology companies.

At the same time, the world is coming to Cape Town for many other reasons. The new International Convention Centre opened in 2003, and massive film studios are nearing completion, confirming the city's status as a business and media hotspot. When World Cup soccer comes to South Africa in 2010, Cape Town will be a major venue.

Like other cities in South Africa, Cape Town has had to face up to the realities of its past and cope with the major difficulties of the present. Progress in many areas such as housing and employment has been agonizingly slow. The city now enjoys one enormous advantage it never had before, however—its many different races are learning to work together on equal terms to build a prosperous future.

◄ *HIV/AIDS awareness was part of the message at the Cape Town Minstrel Carnival held in 2004.*

Time Line

c. 30,000 B.C. The earliest evidence of human culture in the region—San rock paintings in the Western Cape.

c. 50 B.C. Khoikhoi herders arrive in the Cape area.

c. A.D. 500 Bantu-speaking peoples move into southern Africa and probably begin trading with the Khoisan, who are a mixture of the Khoikhoi and San peoples.

1488 Bartholomeu Dias sails around the Cape, which he names "Good Hope."

1503 The first Europeans land on the Cape; Antonio de Saldanha climbs Table Mountain.

1510 The Khoisan and Portuguese battle; seventy-five Portuguese die but the number of Khoisan killed is unknown.

1652 Jan van Riebeeck establishes a Dutch fort and gardens.

1658 The Dutch bring slaves from the East Indies to work on the farms.

1660 Van Riebeeck plants a bitter almond hedge to mark border of European territory.

1685 French and German settlers arrive.

1795 The British seize control of Cape Town.

1814 The Cape officially becomes a British colony.

1834 Slavery is abolished.

1860 Construction work begins on Alfred dock; telegraph line is laid between Cape Town and Simon's Town.

1899–1902 The British and the Boers fight over control of South Africa; the British win.

1910 Cape Town becomes the legislative capital of the new Union of South Africa.

1948 The National Party comes to power in South Africa and introduces the apartheid system of racial segregation.

1952 The African National Congress begins its program of defiance against the South African government.

1964 Nelson Mandela is imprisoned on Robben Island.

1966 The Group Areas Act forces black and Cape Coloured communities to move to Cape Flats.

1983 A mass protest meeting at Mitchell's Plain leads to the formation of the United Democratic Front.

1986 Desmond Tutu becomes the first black archbishop of Cape Town.

1990 Nelson Mandela is released from prison and makes his first speech at Cape Town City Hall.

1994 First free elections; Mandela becomes president of South Africa.

2004 South Africa is appointed host of World Cup Soccer for 2010.

Glossary

apartheid the government system of separate development for different racial groups, aimed at keeping whites in power.

artificial fibers threads made in factories from sources such as petroleum and wood products, which are then woven into cloth.

breakwaters walls or other structures that protect a harbor from the full impact of the sea.

British Empire a huge collection of colonies and dependent countries around the world taken over by Great Britain starting in about 1700.

business park an area exclusively devoted to companies, their offices, and factories

commerce the buying and selling of goods, especially on a large scale.

container one of the large sealed cases used to carry goods by containership or truck.

demonstration a public gathering of people to express a joint opinion or to demand something.

Dutch East India Company a commercial company established in the Netherlands in 1602 to trade with countries in the Indian Ocean and East Indies.

export to sell or to send goods to a foreign country.

garrison a group of soldiers stationed to defend a fortress or town.

Hindus people who believe in Hinduism, a religion of India with many gods and goddesses; Hindus believe that a person is reborn many times into many different lives.

imperialist someone who believes in extending and increasing the power of their country over another country; imperialists often advocate taking over another country.

infrastructure the system of public works, such as roads and electricity, in a region.

metropolitan area the whole extent of a very large or important city.

minaret a tall tower on a mosque; a prayer leader often stands in a minaret to call Muslims to prayer.

multinational company a company that trades and has offices in different countries around the world.

proportional representation a method of deciding the result of an election, by which parties are represented in proportion to their share of the total vote.

racial segregation a policy of keeping different races separate from each other in everything from work and housing areas to bus seating and schooling.

right wing the conservative faction of a political group.

sabotage destroying property or hindering a government's or business' normal actions in an effort to defeat that government or business.

townships black or Cape Coloured residential districts, usually on the outskirts of a town.

treason a betrayal of allegiance to one's own country.

venue a place where special events are held.

Further Information

Books

Binns, Tony, and Rob Bowden. *The Changing Face of South Africa (Changing Face of . . .)* Raintree, 2002.

Downing, David. *Apartheid (Witness to History)*. Heinemann, 2004.

Gibbons, Glenda Anne. *Picture Cape Town: Landmarks of a New Generation (Getty Conservation Institute)*. J. Paul Getty Trust Publications, 1997.

Hamilton, Janice. *South Africa in Pictures (Visual Geography Series)*. Lerner Publishing Group, 2003.

Holland, Gini. *Nelson Mandela (Trailblazers of the Modern World)*. World Almanac Library, 2002.

Kellett, Francisca. *Cape Town (Footprint)*. Footprint Handbooks, 2002.

Parker, Linda. *The San of Africa (First Peoples)*. Lerner Publishing Group, 2002.

Stotko, Mary-Ann. *South Africa (Countries of the World)*. Gareth Stevens Publishing, 2001.

Websites

www.anc.org.za/people/mandela.html
Read about Nelson Mandela's life and the struggle of the peoples of Cape Town and South Africa to end apartheid on the African National Congress site.

www.cape-town.org
Take a virtual tour on the official site for Cape Town tourism or check out the Web cam shots of Table Mountain and Table Bay.

www.cpnp.co.za
You can learn about the fascinating plants and animals at the Cape Peninsula National Park as well as historical background of the area on the park's Web site.

www.gocapetown.co.za
This Web site carries not only tourist information about the area but images of the city as well. You can also learn the lingo of Cape Town.

www.museums.org.za/iziko/social.htm
Learn about South Africa and Cape Town's social history by following the links on the Museums of Cape Town site.

www.odci.gov/cia/publications/factbook/ geos/sf.html
The World Factbook site contains statistics and information on South Africa's history, geography, economy, people, and other topics.

southafrica-travel.net/westcape/capetown_ guide.htm
This tourist guide also gives information on the history, geology, peoples, and climate of Cape Town.

Index